Puppy Stuff by PUPPIES

Written by

Cathy Seabrook, D.V.M. and
Professional Animal Communicator
And PUPPIES

Dedication

We wish to acknowledge our thousands of persons who asked these questions of us, and wished for solid answers from us.

Here in our puppy best, are the words we wish to say to those we love more than life itself.

Yes, it's true, and you heard it right!

You know - nothing but the purity of our love would entice us to so boldly fashion a document like this, that denigrates no dog nor human in the making, merely demonstrates our willingness to include you in our lives so *fully in understanding* that little stands between us now.

There is no stopping of our growth now to fullness of brilliant dog with you.

Love, love, love – Puppies

INTRODUCTION

This book of questions and answers was compiled by asking all available puppies, known as the Collective Consciousness of PUPPIES - and the volunteers were endless!

Enjoy page after page of PUPPIES' carefully constructed messages, brimming with their best ideas for training and addressing behaviors we call 'problems' with such sensible explanations to enlighten us in the understanding of them in puppies' viewpoint.

Puppies' answers are best read slowly, as each word has been carefully chosen to deliver their message to people.

Imagine every word said with wagging tails, for this was my experience in the communication.

I practised veterinary medicine for 30 years prior to becoming a Professional Animal Communicator. This rare combination of skills presents a fullness of understanding that was unimagined to me as a veterinarian, and daily I am honoured and awed by all that is Animalkind.

Published work is available in our children's book called **Heart Hole Piece Named Horse** - a magical story told by my rescue horse Dante, and illustrated by myself. Dante claims to be the world's first story telling horse, and has dedicated the book to the twinkling in all of us. Horse lovers young and old will enjoy the message straight from the horse's mouth! **Heart Hole Piece Named Horse** is available through Amazon.com and other major book sellers.

This book, Puppy Stuff by PUPPIES, is the first of a series of Animal Communication Books by Cathy Seabrook, D.V.M., and other animals are also featured within the series, which includes:

Kitty Stuff by KITTIES
Pony Stuff by PONIES
Survive Saying Goodbye to Your Pet
And
Train Your Horses by Horses

For additional information and delightful messages in questions to and answers from CAT, DOG and HORSE, please visit our animal communication websites.

Our main website is www.drcathyseabrook.com , our CAT and DOG website is www.whatsuppet.com, our HORSE website is www.whatsupvet.com, and our Pet Loss website is www.survivesayinggoodbyetoyourpet.com .

Welcome to the written world of Animal Communication!

Cathy Seabrook, D.V.M.

Puppy Stuff by Puppies

CHAPTER ONE: THE BEGINNING PLACE

CHAPTER TWO: PUPPY CARE

CHAPTER THREE: PUPPY CHARACTER

CHAPTER FOUR: TEACHING PUPPY

CHAPTER FIVE: TELL ME MORE

CHAPTER SIX: WHAT'S THE REAL DEAL HERE?

CHAPTER SEVEN: BEST IDEAS FROM PUPPY

ACKNOWLEDGEMENTS

NOTES

CHAPTER ONE: THE BEGINNING PLACE

How long do you like to stay with Mom?

We need to stay long enough to hear some stories.

We are not so dependent as other kinds of creatures on stories to succeed, for we come with an intention to re-invent our lives with our person.

So we have an open nature already about possibilities.

See how we just jump at the chance to do everything with you, ready for the best bits of life right out of the crate.

So give us some time with Mother, long enough to learn social manners like pushing at the dinner table and being first in line.

Once we can eat we are ready to roll, so to speak, and get on with the game of life that we came for.

What do you think about your littermates?

Oh yes, those guys.

We understand we are not the only dog in the story, but the sooner we separate from our siblings the better, for we thrive best as single puppies with concentrated focus.

Two or a few of us together lacks focus for us in training, and we always suffer for the 'together' nature of training.

We need one on one concentration and devotion if you want us to achieve any sort of potential with our livelihood.

If you care not about our schooling, we still do.

We hate to waste this good brain of ours and like to find a worthwhile job.

It could be anything for some of us, and others have only one purpose in their intention in this physical life.

You had better seek this out if you pick a dog known for certain traits, as we cannot ever overcome the tendencies that come with breed.

This is why we develop into so many types, to create powerful focus in our livelihoods.

Do you know who your person is?

Of course, or persons, as the case may be.

We know generally what to expect but leave room for
plenty of surprises.

Life would be too boring if we knew all the answers.

But we do know of you, and where you will be generally and
when, and we like to delight in our planning how we will let
you know it is us you are looking for.

And you always know when you get it, like a bolt from the blue bopping you on the bean.

"I just had to take him or her home," you say. "I just <u>knew</u>!"

How is this decided?

Well - we get together with you before you get born, and we have this understanding of our party together in certain physical times.

It is so easy, really, to arrange, and we both decide together.

We can never miss each other in these kinds of agreements.

Some of us don't make up our minds so early, and decide that we will choose when we get in a certain situation in our physical existence.

Some just like choices, and some like certainty.

It is easy to simply say, "I am going to let it present itself to me, and then I am going to run with it wherever it takes me."

Such is dog, you know, ready to go at the least suggestion of fun!

Do you get to pick your breed?

Not so much really. We come intending to suit your desire for us if we have made a deal prior to our arrival.

Some of us, if we had trouble past times with physical discomforts, like noses, or eyes, or skin, or feet being too slow to keep up with life, well - then we choose something more brilliant the next time, but only generally, like longer legs, or longer noses, or mixed up breeds for better compliance with health... stuff like that.

There are some, a few only, that return consistently within one breed type and these dogs have excelled so brilliantly in occupation and service to mankind, that to do otherwise would seem pointless to them.

So they always come as the same old skin type. But it suits them best - so whatever!

Some of you come in breeds that have some physical difficulties. Why?

It came linked to a specialty that outshone the difficulty.

Trust we knew when we came that it would be compensated for in heart, or play, or life achievement.

It is not so much really, for we are not so bothered by these little imperfections that cause sniffles, and mucky eyes now and then, or skin dramas or bone ache-ies.

It is all so <u>good</u> really, having had the choice of the greatest things linked to the little niggles.

No big deal, ever!

Do you pick your colour?

We rarely care for colours, and let it fall as it will.

But if you had an arrangement with us and love a certain colour, well - that is built into the agreement for recognition to get us started.

And yes, of course we know colours!

We see all things as God intended and He made beautiful colours. Silly!

Do you pick your occupation?

We do strive to suit occupation in our typing.

Especially with contracts we need to be choosy here.

Hunting dogs have a wide choice, and so do farm dogs.

Lap dogs – well, they go a bit crazy in breed types, so they alone are allowed specific participation by breed.

Some of us have very high career intentions, and we must suit those to a tee, so expect when dogs have powerful roles in service, like Seeing Eye dogs, or herd dogs, or police dogs - those must suit type exactly for fulfillment of their roles with you.

What do you remember from your last time?

Only the odd good bit.

We preserve fun habits for you if we come again to you, and we like certain hobbies, like chewing or jumping, or other distinctive traits that you recognize.

We come smarter and better equipped for conscious involvement with you in a new time frame.

And we always remember love.

You will see this in our eyes from before, and know this without being able to say why properly.

CHAPTER TWO: PUPPY CARE

When do you want to start on solid food?

As soon as our little tummies can't be full with Mother's milk, give us solid food.

We will eat it watered or un-watered, because we understand what our tummies cry for.

As early as 4 weeks, give us something solid to think about and we will be happy little clams for doggies.

How often do you want to eat it?

All the time!

Seriously, we would if you let us, but we understand the pooping reflex comes with meals, so every few hours depending on our size.

The little wee ones need frequent feedings for their sugar requirements.

Us bigger breeds every 3 to 4 hours for sure, until we drift away from the bowl and you find it full.

Then you may feed us less often, but always twice a day until we are about full grown.

It is a routine we thrive on, knowing you have a similar routine, and we always want to do things with you rather than apart.

What about people food?

Oh, those smells entice us right into our deep recesses of our brains, and then we get kibble!

It is an unfairness of the agreement we ponder about - why we agreed to dismiss table food and eat brown bits of goo.

Give us something good in the day regarding food, and we will eat the kibble happily, knowing it is easiest for most of our dear ones.

But when there is spaghetti, or gravy or meat, then please, pretty please add it on top!

Love - Puppies!

What about dog food?

As we said, it is necessary, and food is good for us, and we don't complain much unless it seems to make us sick somewhere, and puppies always love to eat, so we accept all nutrition without regard for its contents.

The rest is up to you, dear ones.

What about bedtime?

We all need lots of sleep to grow.

So for the first while we seem to sleep and eat a lot.

But then we get a bit bigger and sleep is more of a waste of play time.

We need a quiet place to ourselves at first, to drown out the loneliness of Mother gone.

Help us with a special place called bed, in an out of the way place, and we will adapt to it quickly.

Put it in the middle of commotion and we will think commotion is our new life and adapt to that as well!

Put us to bed at <u>night</u> in a crate beside you, so we know someone is alive with us.

Otherwise we seem fine to sleep at naptime in crate or out of it, as long as we know you are available to us on waking.

Bedtime is always best with you, of course. See how we try to weasel under the covers to be right by your heartbeat.

What about whining?

This is our communication tool of polite asking for something we really, <u>really</u> need.

We come unequipped for asking you questions any other way.

It is always important to us, and our purity of thought in the moment, and you know how dog always puts his heart into his moment.

So think of the thing we are asking for as really, really important to us.

We use it lots if we think we must pee or poo, or need out to be with you.

Otherwise, it may be a passing thought if momentary.

If it persists, please just think of us and the thought will appear in your head about what we need.

We have that part worked out ahead of time for us, you see.

So perfectly explained!

Tell me about vet visits.

Treat this like your own doctor, for we depend with our very lives on good communication in this arena, and wish you to establish the best of relationship with this type of person for us.

We do our best once there to win them to us, and puppies shine in the clinic for all to see.

Pick someone gentle in thought and hand and we are most content and satisfied about your choice.

If they know anything about doggies' hearts and minds then the match is complete.

How do I pick the right vet for you?

Find one that matches <u>you</u> for us.

You must get along well for us to have good expectation of our visits.

Girl vets seem to praise us best, and man vets seem to be more practical and unable to squeak as well, but good in heart and minds to us.

Our most boisterous selves like men, and our most timid selves like girls.

Simple, really.

What about getting neutered?

A necessary evil, but too many of us are lost and wandering it seems, so do what you will to minimize the lost-ness for us.

It is really ok and expected now when we live in cities with you.

What about toe nails?

Let them rub off if possible, but if not, for Heaven's sake don't let them break on us! Do something!

What about tail and dewclaw surgeries?

This unfortunate menace to all good puppies is a bad dream to us.

We know it exists in possibility for us, and dread the occurrence, especially when our tails do such magnificent work in the energy realm.

But it is part of our dance with you sometimes, and we accept all parts of the dance, even the stepping on of toes, so to speak.

Do what you will, for it will not last long, this mutilation of a perfectly good puppy - for the veterinarians are rebelling en masse now, and times are a-changing for us.

Whoopee!

What about cosmetic surgery?

Not that – no, never! Breed us better - give us longer noses, less squashed faces, and lids that fit our eyes.

Breed better, breed better, breed better! Have we said enough here on that?!

What about shots?

Necessary today, for some ambivalent viruses exist now with which we cannot agree, nor will they negotiate it seems.

So protect us wee ones, in minute bits and pieces, for our little systems like things spread out.

There is more good in them than bad, dear people - more good.

It is why dogs agree to anything with you, for the good outranks the bad, and in a moment we have forgotten we got a picky and isn't the vet cool giving me so many treats!

Love my vet!

Tell me about worms.

We share a commonality, worms and us, and we mind them not so much really except when they overpopulate and move into stomach, where food and worms don't fit together.

Keep us worm free to grow best, and the worms don't mind the sacrifice to our benefit.

CHAPTER THREE: PUPPY CHARACTERS

What about timid puppies?

Some of us are small in heart, representing the sweetness you crave.

If you win this heart of timid doggy you will have changed your own to match the sweetness.

See how she cowers when you approach or look or even think of her.

Learn to think better then.

Learn to see her brave and big and bold, and you have found the trueness of her heart and stature in this lifetime with you.

Kind, soft, sweet, tender, fragile – now see her powerful queen and goddess, for she is that, come to test your abilities to grow to it in yourself.

What about aggressive puppies?

We come to challenge your leadership obviously.

See what it takes to win this dog's heart for real, to trust him for real, and yes, her too, for the female dog is one to test every fibre of your being if she comes aggressive.

What makes us so? We have not been convinced in prior lifetimes of the value of the trip, and saw more clearly from our position after departing the possibilities for betterment - but now born and being with people we are bereft of memory that launched us here, and now we remain unconvinced of the value in the relationship.

Convince us we are a team of priceless proportions, and then we are one in mind and heart for eternity.

Convince us not, and we will be passed around until we die prematurely, and consider if we return to try again when God explains the reality of the possibilities.

Rarely does this type of doggie remain unconvinced of true purpose with you, so consider the growling an attempt to question the validity of the commitment with us for the most part.

"Will you love me anyway? Will you find a way to bring my best bits forward in this lifetime? We shall see!"

What about dominant puppies?

Well, this is just normal of course.

We all want to be the leader, born in us, and agreed by God, so accept this as just dog-ness.

"Who's the boss today, me or you?!" We try this question out continually.

And sometimes we get that you are, but sometimes we never mind you and do our own thing.

Both are rewarding to us, for we don't mind having a leader if deserving of the position to us.

Do you all like people?

Most of us are people oriented, but some of us come to work more than hug you.

Some people are more likeable than others but all are worthy of the dance with us, and some are chosen for such pure purpose as to out-distance that word into forgetfulness and replace it with unity of soul as Heaven has never seen before.

All serious doggies have these types of agreements in place – deep, soul wrenching, soul helping partnerships that you know when you meet them, and seem to weep an eternity when they are lost.

We are still there, of course, with you - bound for all time in our deep, deep contract of love with you.

Do you like other dogs?

Not so much really ... they are ok.

We are all about the play as we play together happily, but our bonds are lesser than our bond with you.

It is useful for conversation and discussion of course, and teaching is very valuable when allowed by a superior trained individual.

Do you like big animals?

Not so much unless we come to herd them, and then we understand at our base it is about moving them with eye and body stance, and they just get it with us, so it is fun to be so talented with the big ones.

Horses?

No. We don't agree to the drive with them - they have their own rules, but cattle and sheep agreed to the dance in time.

What's the difference in thinking when you come as companion or as working breed?

It goes like this. "Where's my buddy? Where's my buddy? Oh, there you are, adorable you! What are we playing now? What games do you know today? What love will we spill all over the place today dear, adorable, precious soul-mate of mine?"

And,

"The weather's good now to hunt.
The breeze tells me of ducks in the pond over there.
I wait only for the signal, dear Master, to send me flying straight and true to purpose bred so deep in me I live for it.
Send me now! Send me now! Send me now - I beg you!"

See devotion in both, dear friend, as you think of us, for we are charged with our purpose so purely that we cannot think otherwise.

To love, to work, to be with you - it is all mixed up in there together you see, and above all we endear you into our hearts.

Like blood goes you run in us, holding us firm in our contracts and agreements of dance and life and love.

We adore you in love, we adore you in work - we adore you.

See it now?

**What's the difference between purebreds
and mutts-ies?**

Just consistency of sorts. Not so much in temperament as
was once thought, for we have been bred too many times to
retain the beginnings of the breed.

But the look, the bone structure, the hair - that is consistent
now.

And of course you get the things we dragged along, like
dysplasia, or cataracts or other bothersome niggles.

We endeared you with beguiling looks, and you forgot to use common sense and pick the best of us to breed on.

Oh bother!

What's the deal with designer doggies?

Here you see our answer to the above dilemma!

Note our brilliance please.

We took cute on cute, and paired it up, and now the best bits are brought forward again, and the niggles start to wane for us.

It has always been known that purebreds tagged stuff with them, and that mutts-ies had better health, so see these designer mutts-ies for all of that - cute on cute and health to boot!

CHAPTER FOUR: TEACHING PUPPY

How best to house train you?

Well, this can be tricky, for many of us are just not so ready when you take us home, to learn so much at once.

We never had to worry with Mother there. And now so many rules!

Try to be <u>so</u> patient with us, for many of us have no clue.

We just go and there it is - poof! - on the floor and now we hear a lot of loud noises and what's all that about we think, and then we are swooped up in arms and tossed outside, or worse, it must be examined in our very faces, and what does that mean???

It means nothing to us, except to make us think we better run if that happens again, and now we begin to think you can't catch us, and the game is on!

So let us in on this one easy if you can.

Present us the opportunity to go out many, many times every day, no matter what is on the television.

Don't let us learn it is easier not to alert you when we can finally feel it coming.

It is difficult enough to remember what it means as pups to feel we have to go, let alone remember <u>where</u> to go now that we live with you, so help us by paying attention!

We will whine first, then sit down and stand up and look around for where we should do whatever it is that is coming through us.

And we have given you warning, for none of us likes making mistakes with our new people.

Like new-bies fresh from the box, we need understanding and compassion especially with this aspect, for it ratifies our agreement more solidly when we get it fast.

We hope this has helped sufficiently, for many puppies stress out about house training, when we don't even know where the way out is.

Paper?

Well, this is one way to do it.

But start us here and we are here forever, so make up your mind about paper or grass.

Personally, we adore the grass and improve its appearance profoundly (smile)!

What about crates?

Oh, we love crates, hide and seek places, private places, hiding places and sleeping places!

Never worry about our attachment to our little rooms, but only remember that you have placed us there when you return and we have been waiting ALL day for you to come back to us.

Never use them as a barricade when you are home please, only when necessary to keep us safe if you have gone somewhere.

What do you want to know about how to get outside?

Where is the door?

How do I get your attention off that thing and onto me?

Will it be barking? Then teach me to be noisy.

Will it be peeing in front of you? Then forget about me.

Will it be scratching? Then teach me to damage your door frame.

Show me the path.

Show me how the door opens with a tap-tap-tap of my paw, and we are onto the best-est, quietest, gentlest path to a lifetime of politeness asking to be let out and in.

Don't show me and I will figure out a way to get you jumping when I need out, and the more rude my asking, the faster you seem to move to help me!

Leaving you alone when we work.

Never leave us if you can help it.

We are lost without you as puppies.

And this often interferes with our training, delaying us in understanding due to necessity of 'accidents' when we are all alone.

Arrange for help for us, to avoid us feeling retarded about elimination skills ... please.

Leaving you alone – ever?

As we said, we come to be with you.

If at all possible let us be there at your feet, or in your seat, or adoring you with our big brown eyes.

Leave us, and we may go mad, if not primed properly.

Many dogs seek this demonstration now, having intended something else for their time with you, and it nearly drives them outside their mind with distress at lack of fulfillment of contract.

Somehow we will get your attention, and this seems to remind you that we are desperate alone without you.

Some of you get this, and some of you don't obviously, or the behavior would not exist now.

Best time to teach you about collars and leashes.

As soon as you get us you should get us used to this, but gently, for our little necks are fragile as wee ones, and never withstand pulling.

It just dulls us to the lead to pull on us, and we beseech you to find a better psychology for teaching us to lead with you.

See how we pull you around so you get the idea here.

Be non-gentle with us and we will be non-gentle back, as a rule.

Some of us though, never give you a chance and just run with you, knowing the running is more important for now than the listening.

These types need significant leadership balanced with benevolence of thought and psychology.

We will challenge you in your gut of guts to love us even, to make you realize your inadequacy in leadership.

If you have this kind of contract with us, expect to be challenged but in the challenging find the things that fix us and you together.

When we are gentle doggies you have found the very thing you sought and now we let up and you think we behave, but you just found what <u>you</u> needed in us.

Never think we are purposeless in our pulling on you, for we drive you to a better place of thought about growing with us in relationship, and if you love us solidly enough we always win-over the behavior.

It is our decree to you we are worth the effort to adjust to a better match in thought and physical aids.

**When we tell you sit and stay,
what are you really understanding from us?**

Well - we get that you mean something sort of important, but it is incongruent to our nature to sit and stay when life calls us so brightly from every corner.

So we may struggle a bit in understanding why any doggie would be required to do something so mundane.

But we do endeavor to please, for that is dog at his base, and so we entertain the thought of figuring it out long enough for the thing in your hand that is enticing us to <u>move</u> - to sit.

So we get there are simple school rules applied here, but if started too young to 'stay' we lose interest in figuring that one out, and so it is the most difficult concept for young puppies to get.

We know you get our drift here.

What about puppy classes?

We understand we must go to school to fulfill some purpose and be amenable to living together.

So take us later, when we have had a chance to go to earth school and family school a bit longer, and digest necessities before stretching our minds into more rules.

We think 8 weeks is good for home school and 16 weeks for puppy school.

Save bigger schools for year time only, when we have digested sufficiently the other teachings.

What about agility classes?

We love these but must be able to cope with beginning places and spaces first.

Expect by 8 months we could begin some lessons, but never work us until we are one fully, or our bones will not be best for our lifetime.

What about real jobs like herding or Seeing Eye dogs?

We need sufficient time to adjust to these demands of significant work, which involves not only physical but intense spiritual commitment that we have deemed worthy to accomplish in our lifetime in this era.

We still need to be puppies so don't rush us into this too completely, too quickly.

Always allow lots of play with not commanding, or we will forget some of our greatness related to fun.

Leave the fun in these occupations and you will have the best of dog, as service and joy at your side.

What about hunting jobs?

We revel in the hunt of course, as so many of us intend to partake, which you recognize by the hunting breeds available.

Early on we demonstrate to you our capacity in this realm, and are more eager than most to begin what we inherited into this occupation, for there is history steeped in these breeds that hunt and it permeates their meagre intentions as mere soul companions, elevating the hunting dog to true working aide and valuable workman.

Regard hunting puppies' breeds as the reality they present, providing sustenance on all levels for their masters.

It is an honour to serve in this capacity, nearly forgotten compared to previous lifetimes when the dogs ruled the roost in home and cottage.

What about loving jobs?

This is the supreme aim of course, to excel in this premise, and thus so many doggies come smaller now, to fit every need and kneecap.

All dogs have this aspect to them, but the working dogs less so, and less *more* so in the wilder counterparts bred more closely to wolf ancestors.

Wolf ancestor dogs simply have not known this aspect as clearly, and do not cling to it or expect better than wild from life to life.

Only when they learn of it at some point in a random encounter with a chance person, will they consider such a thing exists between canine and companion.

Then there is no stopping them, these wild dogs that have not known love, for never again will they settle for the wildness over the love - it is done for them for all time, and now they come as Chihuahuas and Beagles and Spaniels and such, eager to indulge in all the love that contracts bring, now that they know they exist.

Lucky is the wildest part of dog to discover this, and precious is the soul who teaches it to him.

What about our voice tone?

Well, sometimes you think if you sound mad that we get it better, that we were bad or something like that.

But see that there is no bad in dog.

There is only your idea of behavior that you formed for us, and we have nothing to do with that after all, and are simply innocent bystanders, momentarily mirroring your distress at something impossible to comprehend for us.

So we mirror your sounding mad for bad but it is only a mirror, saying, "See how you look and feel inside about what you are thinking about me, the doggie that adores you."

It is such a mismatch you see, to think you could make dog feel bad about anything to do with you, for we only see the best bits of you for the most part, and ignore what doesn't matter to us, which is everything else.

So growl at us if you must, and we will mirror the exact thing you need to stimulate thought in you to change that tone or thought about us which is incorrect, incongruent and impossible for us to believe you could think about such an excellent, precious being sent to love you!

What about learning to swim?

Don't you dare throw us in, for we will remember the survival desperation of the moment for that lifetime!

If we must swim, allow us in - and that means the first few days we might only look.

Let the water invite us to dream with it, and off we go, confident in our safety and playtime there.

Some of us would never accept the invitation of course!

What about learning to pull?

Well, we get the fun of this game so clearly, but you teach us not to pull on collar, and then ask us to pull in harness - so for some of us we just need to learn to pull to avoid a conflict in command here.

Those of us who pull revel in it, glory in it and live for it.

What about police and service work?

This work has such a serious nature to it that many of us shudder at being chosen for this type of work environment.

There seems to be too little play in this work effort area, and most must be born into it, coming with such knowledge of this line of business that they settle for mostly work and little play, so opposite of puppy intentions.

So see these puppies as serious puppies in your choosing of us to work like this, and try to remember we came for the <u>fun</u> of it somewhere in there please!

What about farm and herding work?

Oh, to be chosen for this line of work is treat indeed - for we dance with the creatures that agreed to dance with us, and nothing is more satisfying than partnership in this realm.

See this as instinctive for most - the herding, the collecting, the gathering of huge beings at a glance from our wary, keen eyes - burning holes in their hides if they hesitate.

It is such a delight to come forth with this in mind, and you bet we come equipped for this action, and people see it in us right off the bat!

What about medical work like seizures?

These are the most elite of specialties here, detecting imbalances in energy so minutely as to awaken a person and let them know a crisis intervention is needed immediately.

These dogs come with full intention to delight in this offering, so it is work and it is fun, and so rewarding to have this talent fostered for them.

Most dogs can do this, if treated as potential medical servants.

All it takes is an introduction and we sense the thing we know is wrong and blaring at our energy readers.

What about treats?

Oh, the expectation that shimmers as we anticipate the thing you hold in your hand or pocket.

We wonder about the giving of it - what it involves, or is it free!?

Maybe it's free! And we bounce and be-bop beside you in the sheerest of joy, and you laugh and offer it all the sooner!

Best treats.

Anything you love we will love, but spare us the dark chocolate, of course.

Need one every time you do something good?

Of course we do, or why should we behave and be allowed to be distracted from our great play to dance with you in games you prefer over ours?

Treat us for our participation and you will gain our eagerness in the game you make, and lose the treats and you will see our distraction calls us louder. Simple!

Do you prefer to have an older dog teach you?

Always best if we have work to do that they already know, for nothing beats a sincere, benevolent mentor.

Pair us with a goof and we become one, pair us with a hunter and we become one, pair us with a runaway ... well, you know the rest the story.

CHAPTER FIVE: TELL ME MORE!

Tell me what a walk means?

We greet the day, and salute the dawn and grass and sun and wind.

It is where we connect the best to all we came from and where we go next.

Spare us your blathering about why you can't walk us, for it does the same for you as for us.

Notice how we make you go to connect back up to more of <u>you</u> that you've been missing.

It is the thing, dear ones, we crave most.

Walk with us now and we become the thing together - the past, the present, the future meanderings - it all bonds us like glue.

Tell me about kids and puppies.

Well, this is the best scenario ever - two infectious, magic, shiny objects dancing together, lit up for all to see.

But see that we are old enough not to bite them, for the draw with kids in enchanted is deep-set.

If they move fast we chase and if we chase we bite - simple really.

So teach them the games with us for best results - like ball throwing and running together on line.

Children's hearts beat with ours and we hear it when we are together.

We quicken to match it and are one in the game.

Tell me about cars.

The draw to these monsters is unexplainable even to us.

We see them as the thing to catch and conquer, chase from our place, and rule supreme.

We have no teaching of them except what you show us.

So teach us well the dangers, for we know there are great dangers unexplained to us but resonating on the ethers.

Walk us up to them and hold within your hands which touch our leads the expectation of <u>caution</u>.

Cock your head if you must to help you find it, and we will see you wonder about the very thing you wish us to wonder about.

So simple, really, to teach dog, for we understand and mimic you so completely in actions.

Explain the thing is not safe for puppies and to stay away now little ones.

Sit with us a moment and see us well in the yard with you, holding the yard picture in your minds as long as possible.

Then spin and give us a grand play there to reinforce its delight to us!

Now we have what we really needed, the focus place where play lives! Who needs to go where the cars go?

What about chasing cars?

They move, we run - it is nature's dance with predator and prey.

Big prey is no different of course, and off she goes and we are away without our noticing we have left really.

That chase reflex so takes over our being, that before we can think we have moved, and it has enticed us onto road or under truck, but enticed us it has.

So help us with this enticement to be drawn to danger, and imagine for us a better space in the beginning, teaching us safety in yard or park, always <u>hesitating for us in</u> <u>stride</u>

when cars approach and we will get the meaning in your gait.

"Wait," it says to us. "Assimilate the danger here, and regard the thing you see as prey as something to avoid."

"Play here," you call to us now, and we are not enchanted in the chase now, only beguiled by the dance in your feet and the chant in your voice to focus chase on <u>you</u>!

What about riding in the back of a truck?

Oh, to be king of the road with you, owning the speed and wind and smells and stories blasting in our faces as we bounce around on slippery surfaces and the like, all for the joy of going with you into wonderland.

Can you tell we delight like no other thing in this ride with you, dear friends?

What about sticking your head out the window?

Blasted with stories and breezy tales, we revel in this behavior, and little rivals it for glee in the car.

What about toys?

TOYS! We crave, we dig, and we love our toys, and the more, the merrier - the worse for wear, the lovelier - and the bigger, the better!

Provide them, or we find other things that you might not name the same.

What about cats?

Cats - the teachers of respectful space.

We all know and dread the swatting cat, but it takes one swat and our memories shove to the forefront and we remember the lesson - mostly.

Some of us are so friendly we think to overcome this gracious monster by sweetness and light, and she is not having of that, so we try and try again.

It is the dance we agreed to before time began, and in the end we will love each other in our ways, and sometimes be one in the finding.

What about being tied up?

We hate this!!! Don't do it ever!

Of course, we accept that we might get hurt if we wander off, but minimize this safety tie the best you can, and give us freedom mostly.

We accept the tie deal for you to feel we are safe and out of danger or trouble, as you call it, but it represents a lost link to us where we are unconnected physically and mentally.

You will hear our cries of disconnection, thinking we bark at the moon.

It is a cry for connection and to re-establish our purpose with you.

See how some need heavy chains to keep them home, which represents the degree of separation between us and you.

What about crowds of people?

When we are young this distraction befuddles us and sometimes distresses us greatly, for we have not the knowledge that maturity knows of being safe and ok with strangeness.

It is enough at first to meet and greet all the family knows, but to be thrust into a teeming populace of unknown is too much for most puppies to handle.

Take us gently into places where crowds gather - keep it quiet and simple for us, and not too long please.

And when we show you we are more capable, then stay longer until it becomes normal for us to endure the commotion.

Trust we never like crowds so much until we have our commands down pat and trust our <u>own</u> behaviors.

We expect to participate, but take it easy on our introduction, that is all we ask of you.

What about being with other dogs?

Other dogs either distract us or teach us, so pick our mates carefully for behavior, for we shall strive to be exactly like them in all regards.

It is up to you if you choose more doggies in the fold, and we will show you the result very quickly to address with us, or not.

Dogs like dogs, dogs have trouble with some dogs, and dogs love people best.

We relish undivided attention, but do not despise you for dividing yours amongst those you love.

Dogs or no other dogs, it is all alright.

What about puppy mills?

We have a comment here on this situation, but it is very, very serious now.

Most people dread this word, but in fact puppy mills provide puppies to people who need puppies.

And the sorrier we look the better we are taken care of, and the prouder people seem to have rescued us from such a start.

It is, no matter, a start, and all puppies crave a start somewhere.

We know not the difference it seems, whether puppy mill, or backyard breeding, or shelter of lost - we all begin somewhere and know our stories with you.

So it is but a short wait to find you generally, and nothing we begrudge our beginning with.

See it as the place our love story began, for your intention with us overrules our memories so completely once we find you, all we think of is our 'now' with you, not the 'then' before, which is blurred already with tears of happiness in our hearts.

What about shelters?

These places do us great aide, always.

Never think it is any other way for us, for we see their light glowing from afar, often wondering how to reach the place through the traffic and jumble that is civilization.

Gradually we 'be found' to get there.

The people there are meant to exist as beacons of care for us, and once we get there, sometimes we think to move on to a new purpose and home, and sometimes we have seen enough and landing in a care zone is sufficient for us to decide to take the leap <u>back</u> home.

If we did not want to accept the possibility of the leap offer, we would not end up there - we have that much say and that much choice.

We only get found if we choose it.

What about dog parks?

This little gem of an oasis primes us for re-living in cities.

We crave the grass under our feet, and revel in our outings to these places.

Make sure we know some commands so we are safe with the bigger dogs, but as soon as we can go safely take us for a romp.

You will have our undying appreciation for this gift to city dog - the *leaving of pavement feel* in our paws is a godsend to us.

We adore our park adventures.

CHAPTER SIX: What's the real deal here?

What about peeing when we say hello?

Oh this. Well, it happens you know. Sheesh!

Seriously, we all try so darn hard to do the right thing when we are introduced, or out at a party, or visiting our friends, and we worry about the circumstance, and the strangeness and the bigness of hellos, and there we have wet ourselves and you comment and we think something is wrong for sure, and worry all the more the next time.

It becomes normal to worry and respond this way when greeted or at a new place or with someone new.

As natural as it is, it seems unaccepted.

So this is what you do to help us with this little bit of peeing.

Ignore us when we pee. Don't comment about us peeing. Pretend we didn't pee. Let it dry before you notice it.

It is not real. It isn't significant.

See how I adore you so completely - you are my shining hero knight of lights, and my heart is so stuck on you we will conquer anything we set our minds to.

See me for my greatness, not my snivelling submissive behavior as you call it - see me for heart and soul and light and shining self - reflection of God that I am in your life.

And now, I am done with peeing for good, for I have been recognized for what I truly am - a magnificent, brilliant being, called your dog.

There - complete!

What about humping people's legs?

We crave sexual interaction - we are dogs!

We smell and dream and enjoy nature, and you have nature stuck all over you - and sometimes we just take part more powerfully in the nature of 'us' selves.

No offence! Always laughed at - always talked about - always noticed.

The most boisterous of our kind think it becoming and enchanting and a complement of the highest sorts.

Not so sure you always agree, but we are often immune to the condemning energy as the hysterical nature of the response to the behavior overrides any negative inflection.

What about porcupines?

These prickly pear things come with no warnings to us, appearing as enticing little wanderers, rattling and drawing us with an aura of pretending to be invisible - for nothing bothers them in reality and they unobtrusively scoot here and there, regarding none but themselves.

And then we appear and have to stick our big noses onto the rattling bits, and there we have gone and done it, innocent as we are, and there is hell to pay for our inquisitiveness!

What about digging up stuff?

Treasure, treasure, treasure - enhanced by dirt and grime and nature, all the better for the rubbing around in it, and appealing to us, calling us, from two feet underground!

We smell it, we breathe it in as story, and we go for it.

It calls us, you see, so what else would we do but answer it?

What about chewing rocks?

Rocks were made for dogs alone, and we name them like babies and special toys.

They have a feel unlike anything else, so solid a part of all that is for us, and we play together in the knowledge of the soundness of it all, the solidity of rock being like our attachment to you for us.

"Solid, solid, solid - oh rock of my mine, come play and tease and dance with me, for I have known you forever, as you have know me." We are two creatures so divinely designed by God himself, to represent the firmest connection to Him in physical and heart.

What about chewing bones?

Bones are solace to us - representing stories of sacrifice for the continuance of man and animalkind.

We revel and worship and honour the giving in the chewing and thinking related to bone.

See how rewarding it seems when nature begets more in nature, as mineral and ash become part of us.

It is a reciprocal thanksgiving for contribution to time before us, and we just honour the giving of life to life, that's all.

What about chewing period?

Well, now we get to business here.

What a hysterical delight this is to us, grinding our timeless jaws on unforgiving objects, growing our teeth big and strong, and giving us stimulus for thought.

For there is no better time to grow in mind than when we chew.

See it as proper training for an exceptional mind - the movement seems to send blood to our brains like no other activity.

Born to chew, and some never recover from the puppyhood drive and wreck havoc with teeth their whole lives!

What about garbage?

Now we get to the nitty gritty temptation of all times for us.

Always, **<u>always</u>** there is something grand in garbage - and always worth the salvage and commotion you make afterwards!

It is impossible to outrank garbage in appreciative energy, and you can't get negative enough about it to affect us, and so it is untrainable for you.

Restrict access is the only option, and then we will seek it out on the curbs at other houses if at all possible!

What's good about socks and shoes?

Everything - smell, taste, feeling - succulent sock-ies and shoes-ies to us!

As good as being on your lap or knee, or at your feet of course!

The stories in shoes are in smell for us, telling us how you spent your day on earth away from us.

The socks are more intimate, reminding us of tickle toes and tender times.

Just fun really - all for fun, always!

What about eating poop?

Oh that - the story telling behavior - enticing us, drawing us
with a tale of another being, or tale of our own being –
smack, smack, smack!

"Hm. So that's what I ate that made me so delighted. I
remember it now, the very smell and taste I liked so much.
Look there's more of that - let's try this piece over here."

And so, on and on it goes, us reading stories from guts-ies that remind us of good things before-hand.

You do the same in books, and memories.

See it like that, quite innocent really, just dog remembering stuff he or she liked - and liked.

What about licking our faces?

We love you. Simple!

Don't you want to be kissed?

What's with the hiccups?

It means we got a stimulus from our insides that
interrupted normal confluence into the stomach area.

Like there was a roadblock in a nerve, and it bumped into
it.

It really is hysterical to us how you love to see us
hiccupping so big we jump every time we make the noise.

There is great comfort in this saying "hiccup and grow", for indeed it represents to us the same thing, and is harmless and funny at the same time.

Enjoy our antics, for they do not last long, and soon you never hear them from us again!

What about sleeping on our bed?

Never was there such a softie spot as the one next to your feet in bed with you.

Precious sounds of breathing and precious smells of feetsies - nice reminders of physical life with you, absent when not in bed there too, with you.

We see it as a place of refuge, and also king-man-ship, for no-where else do you spend so much time in stillness and quiet.

In your busy lives, at least you rule in sleeping places.

We sometimes forget it is your rule of course, having spent soft times there without you, and it can be a challenge to take over our spot!

Some of us take this to the nth degree, and never let you in with us!

What about riding in the car?

This can be unfortunate for many, as our little tummies rock and roll so much with the movement and uncertainty in the car.

Suddenly our dinner has left us, and we are swerving violently right or left and thrown forward as you stop the car, and sometimes hurl us outside.

Yes, it is comical as you shout to us – "Don't puke in the car!"

We strive to behave, you know, but little tummies don't take the movement well, and many struggle, as you would on a boat in stormy seas.

It is no different of course, in cars.

Try to minimize our trips for us when we are wee ones, and medication is acceptable for trips to help us both recover from the effects of being car sick!

What about eating gross stuff?

Well - nothing is that gross to us - it's simple!

We love the smells of putrefaction, and it draws us in a
dance of delight in stories and promise of amusements.

For it normally comes back to haunt you, more than us, as
our tummies decide whether it will stay on board, or not.

There is always something good in something bad, you see,
serving to cleanse our systems at least, and toughen our
bodies' response to germs.

Dogs always knew this trick, to make us stronger and able to survive on things other species cared not for.

Lately, though, not so many doggies remember the usefulness of this act, and get so stuck on canned and created foodstuffs that one lick of delicious rottenness serves to send their tummies hurling.

It was a useful practice and we carry it on, knowing its historical value to dogs.

What about rolling on gross stuff?

This is splendid perfume to us, full of ripe stories and others' adventures.

We roll to take part in the event, though past.

It is neither good nor bad to us, how we smell, for we are reading a depth of story in our noses that is impossible to explain to people, who long lost their sense of smell to any degree.

We understand you can't get this behavior, which is the funnest and funniest thing to us, in its partaking and your reaction to it!

What's up with sniffing bums?

Well! Here we go on about the true handshake event for dog-dom, where we read about your life in such expansive details of what you ate, who you ran with, how you reacted to your dinner, how your body is working for you, and so much more.

We read it like a book of your day or week, and then there is little worth in fighting or talking, or bothering with social graces, for we know all we need to know and argue about ahead of time - and generally it prevents an argument, because the points are already made in the statement of tail and under-tail events.

What about baths?

Ewh.

Spare us slippery events that worry us in balance.

Spare us degreasing of precious stories all over our backs and paws.

And spare us your pity as we relent not in resenting and repelling of the act that reduces dog to bare naked scent.

What about hairdos?

We always knew our capacity to draw you in with grandiose hair, and some of us overdid it in the breeding shed.

So we go to people who like to play with hair, and it serves us with great purpose as a rule.

Always ensure we can see, and we have the best of hair and sight.

What about that ball?!!

The ball is the THING you see, the game, the target, the opponent, the little scurrier running from the big doggy - and we revel in the chase like it was a rat in the castle.

Go! Go! It teases us! Catch me if you can! And we are off on an adventure of glee and compromise, as it bounces, or gets lost, and then calls us not!

Such a playmate ball is - as happy in the chase as we!

CHAPTER SEVEN: BEST IDEAS FROM PUPPY

Best training ideas for walking.

Take us everywhere.

Let us have some free walking where we can just go safely at our own pace, and then ask us to behave at your side.

For if you ask us first when the draw of life is calling, we will have such difficulty cooperating with you.

Let us have some lead space when we are young, for there is plenty of time to learn to heel, as you say it.

Long lines for puppies are best, where you can reel us in if we stray too far or into danger, and we get to move our chubby little legs freely, exploring the spaciousness of the life we landed in.

Once we are too pooped to pop, now ask us to walk like little gentleman and lady dogs beside you, and we will get it so much easily.

Tired puppies want to stay with you, hoping for naptime.

Busy puppies don't let that word enter the game frame.

Best ideas for coming.

Oh, this one is tough for us if we get the idea that the world is a bigger draw than your reward!

Teach us that come means relief, come means play, come means food, come means petting and any other niceties you can pair it with.

Teach it to us continuously without working at it by saying it relentlessly when we come to you.

It will be the most natural thing in the world to obey once we no longer see it as a command to discontinue our playing elsewhere.

It must be a positive experience or we will choose to ignore you with this precious life saving word.

Come means 'cheesie' – yes, sweetness in our ears.

Make it so and you have us hooked for life on that four letter word.

Best training ideas for not jumping.

OK – well, we knew this was coming didn't we.

Your faces attract us with your bright eyes and sparkly smiles, and we cannot help ourselves.

It is a draw unlike any other part of you, this face you wear, for it represents to us our completeness in contentment contracts - the smiles you wear when we bring you delight.

This is why we came of course, to bring delight to you.

So the reward is on your face, and the nearer we are to it the better we feel about ourselves!

Dogs always feel so good about themselves and only being near your face trumps it for us.

Try to understand the depth of complement to be jumped on - we will never jump on anyone we don't like.

This is how you tell who the good ones are in your life!

Best training ideas for not biting us.

You taste good, you feel good, and you make delightful noise when we bite you - like little squeaks of things we would have killed as wolf.

So delightful those squeaks are to us, reminding us of heritage so deep in dog.

Some of us have this tendency in the forefront and struggle to contain it, especially when you have no strategy to help us with our teething issues.

Find something to encourage us to use instead of you.

And bad tasting things – well, they work but have more negative connotations than taste to us, rather presenting a lack of understanding of our message here.

Try to see it as the one thing that reminds us of history - the squeal, the blood, the hunter in dog that was so long ago.

So honour the history, saying,

"Thank-you for your history, sweet pet of mine. Now this is what you must do since I honoured you. Honour my skin back to me. For I am a tender, fragile creature, delicate in all senses compared to your history, and worthy of honourable treatment. Chew anything but me, for I am Master you see, and in return you will be honoured all your lifetime at my side."

Say it to us – really! And see how we look at you with our big puppy eyes and cock our heads, and you will know you hit a chord deep within us of better things than history ahead.

It will work for all puppies when said with integrity and meaning.

See that we are slightly tired so we can pay best attention, and then tell us that out loud, and slowly or quickly, the biting will cease, but surely, it will.

What about barking?

We must speak of course, as you must, and play makes us bark all the more as you respond to it by asking questions, and, "Yes," we say, "Now you understand!"

All creatures communicate, so never begrudge us our voice, splendiferous in its resonance, shrill in its penetration of space and place.

Annoy us not with yours and we will annoy you not with ours.

See how difficult it becomes to be quiet, and you will appreciate our stance regarding voice sharing.

What about growling?

The games begin, of course, with growling, and continue if we decide we are the better being.

Try to teach a growling puppy another way and he will growl all the more at you!

Beware of those of us so tempted to defer to this behavior, for we know it grows if unaddressed.

We cannot help it, those of us who use it so vehemently, for we have come from a less considered space before hand, not able to think better of a life for ourselves from what we knew before, but hoping to be different and shown the way.

For those of us who growl and scare you, this is the best way to help us consider an alternative lifestyle approach.

Stare at us with benevolence, for we have not known that before.

Think in your heart and minds and say quietly or loudly, calmly and as lovingly as you can muster to this little bear of a creature that barred its teeth and looked at you with contempt and disdain.

"I am your Master wee one. No matter how you speak to me, I am so. It is for you alone I will be the powerful leader you seek, the powerful kindness you crave, and the powerful heart you deserve."

Now sit with us, quietly, and do nothing more.

Wait for us, for it will sink in slowly to us doggies never knowing such character and king and queen-man-ship, and then go on about our business as if we never spoke of it.

Now it is planted in us - us little rotters specializing in growling at you, our benefactors, and we can't help but wonder at the generosity of heart that loves us in spite of ourselves!

In fact, it will shake us to our doggy core, for it is what we have known as <u>our</u> deepest self, for all eternity - that we love despite your issues, your growling, your actions.

And to see it come back to us will shake us into recognition of our true purpose with you.

Trust it will be so, for we are all capable of knowing all that is dog in ourselves.

Some of us just need help in the finding place of it.

Best guidelines for training puppy.

See us as individuals and address our natures first.

We do not all respond to the same type of training - in fact some of us never respond to traditional training - for we have come with great purpose to teach you compliance with different temperaments, to grow that within you to your contracts with us.

For example, some of you are timid, and you select a sweet puppy who turns out to be a holy terror, to teach you to command like a general.

You must become with us the thing to balance your personal self, and the training will demand it of you.

We wait with glee while you struggle to deal with us, as we come up with new challenges all the time.

But in the end you will win, because we try so hard for you, and won't let you give up on our deal.

So each puppy will show you what works best, by responding or ignoring.

If ignoring, think smarter about how we think then, and you will form an idea that seems preposterous, likely the opposite of all you have learned, and figure a way to present it to us - and lo and behold we behave!

Now you have crossed the line into genious dog person and we did it with you. Oh, we are so proud of us then!

So see your challenging doggies as great and wondrous teachers designed to bring out the best of your brains in our dealings, and the best of your emotional commanding forces, retraining your reaction to *considered imagination* in dealing with us, your little beloved rippers, who smile at you secretly as you frown in disgust at our non-response.

We can't <u>not</u> smile, for you are doing so splendidly we think, in this weirdness of doggy-hood we present.

It is all in love of course, but trust us to teach what you need us to teach, for we came to be what you need us to be in all things, not just cuddles and support believed possible in history.

We are more than that now, having evolved with you into conscious mannerisms and relationships - more than dog was, and always improving.

See how we explain to you now the unexplainable!

What is your favorite part about being puppy?

We are one in time and space and eternity - just us two wee bits of stars and moon and sun, dance and song and delight, and doggy kisses, tail smiles and heart gazes.

Puppy! Never in all the world has there been a match for the glee that is us, in you.

Do we have a favorite part? Let's see. It must be you. It is you! It is you! It is you!

Never in our lifetimes have we been so enchanted, so entranced, so fulfilled as when we find you, dear precious bits of light, and Heaven is laughing as we wiggle in your arms and your smile sends radiance for fourteen miles in every direction.

Yes that far, easily! For our arrangement is a Heaven match like no other - NO OTHER!

It is new and fresh and brimming with spirit dream possibilities, and there we are in it because of you.

Thank-you for letting me be your puppy! I will love you forever in this thankfulness - you will see!

Never has there been love like mine for you, dear, dearest soul mate of mine, and never again will such love match it.

Love, love, love – PUPPIES

The End of this Book

Acknowledgements

A special thank-you to PUPPIES for answering my questions so brilliantly and to all the puppy models who asked to be included in the booklet – you are adorable!

Thank-you to our readers and puppy lovers everywhere, who inspired the questions.

We hope you have enjoyed our book.

Cathy Seabrook, D.V.M. and PUPPIES

NOTES

Dr. Cathy Seabrook graduated with Honours from the Ontario Veterinary College in 1981. She practised Equine and Small Animal Medicine for 30 years, and graduated as a Professional Animal Communicator from Animal Spirit Network in 2011.

Please join us at our websites:

www.whatsuppet.com

www.whatsupvet.com

www.drcathyseabrook.com

www.survivesayinggoodbyetoyourpet.com

Thank-you!